WHY DIDN'T I THINK OF THAT?

A Guide
to Better Ideas and Decision Making

A FABLE BY
ROGER L. FIRESTIEN, Ph.D.

INN

WIL   NEW YORK 14231
WWW.ROGERFIRESTIEN.COM

Library of Congress Catalog Card number: 98-92549

ISBN 1-891741-00-4

Cover Design: Pat Edmonds, Left Coast Design.
Layout: Shane Ewald

Firestien, Roger L., 1955-
    Why didn't I think of that? A guide to better ideas and decision making.
ISBN: 1-891741-00-4 (soft cover)
1. Creative ability in business. 2. Problem Solving. 3. Leadership.

Printed in the United States of America

To the wonderful creative spirit
in all of us.

Acknowledgements

Albert Einstein was once quoted as saying, "If you can't say it simply, you don't know it well enough." This has been my goal: to simplify many of the concepts and techniques developed over the last forty years in the field of creativity and innovation. These techniques are designed to help you become deliberately creative, to come up with ideas and solutions to problems when you need them...instead of leaving creativity to chance.

These concepts did not originate with me. As in any work, one stands on the shoulders of many giants. The concepts in this fable build directly on the work of the late Alex F. Osborn. Other concepts are based on the work of Sidney J. Parnes, Ruth B. Noller, Edward deBono, George Prince, and William J. J. Gordon. I'm grateful to them.

I would particularly like to thank Tracey Jung for the concept of "black and white;" John P. Gaulin for several important insights that led to the germination of this book; Lars Hjalmquist for his faith and enthusiasm for this project; and Susan Griffin and Michael Zich for their valuable assistance with the final drafts of the manuscript. Special thanks also to my colleagues Ed Zilewicz, Mary Murdock and the publisher of the first edition, Ted Callisto. Thanks also to Jobie.

This book is dedicated to you and your ability to become more creative and effective in dealing with challenges and opportunities so that you can lead a happier, more prosperous life.

Enjoy!

Foreword to the Second Edition

I haven't always been a business partner of the author, Roger L. Firestien, Ph.D., and I haven't always had a financial stake in the success of this book. There was, in fact, a time when I could have offered a completely unbiased testimonial of the material that's packaged in this book. I would have volunteered to tell you that I think it is one of the best books about creativity on the market.

I would have told you that other books are longer and have better illustrations and larger publishers. But I have yet to see one that packs so much into such an easy, fun-to-read format. I have yet to see one that offers such valuable, powerful advice in such an honestly simple way. The lessons are easy to learn and can be understood quickly by the young, the young-at-heart, and the (as my father would say) chronologically enhanced. Although, like most things in life worth embracing, the concepts require work to master.

However, with such a clear, clever, memorable way of communicating these concepts, you'll soon be grasping the concepts and applying them. And before you know it, you'll be saying, "I bet you wish you'd thought of that" with a vicious, angry sneer. OK, if you sneer, you haven't mastered the concepts here. But you'll definitely be on your way to being deliberately more creative.

Yes, once I would have told you this without having the burden of a "conflict of interest" accusation thrown at me. So I can't say these things now. But I will say, in as much honesty as

I can personally muster, that if you own this book, you'll be contributing to getting Roger L. Firestien, Ph.D. a new, better-looking pair of shoes. Trust me, he needs them.

In the meantime, happy reading, and rest easy in the knowledge that if you assimilate what's contained in this book, you'll soon be saying, "I *did* think of that!"

Jonathan Vehar
Vice-President / Partner
Innovation Systems Group
Senior Partner
New & Improved

CHAPTER ONE

Tyler awoke to the familiar buzzing of his alarm clock. He rolled over, opened his eyes, and stretched. He glanced at the stark, white walls of his room. Gazing out the window, he noticed the gray clouds. It was another gray day—a day just like every other day. He pushed back the white sheets and pulled himself out of bed. He shuffled into his bathroom and took a shower in his white bathtub. Then he patted himself dry with his white bath towel. He washed his face with white soap and brushed his teeth with white toothpaste. Walking back to his bedroom, he plopped on his bed and pulled on his black socks and gray pants. He buckled his belt, tied his black shoes, buttoned his white shirt, tied his black tie, and slipped into his gray jacket.

He wandered into his kitchen and sat down for his usual breakfast of black coffee, a bowl of gray oatmeal, and two slices of white toast. He gazed out at the gray day and thought about the upcoming weekend. Then he realized...it was Tuesday—nowhere near the weekend. He got up from the table, pulled on his black overcoat, and was off to catch the train for another day of work at The Big Black and White Company.

On his way to the station, Tyler stopped to pick up his daily black-and-white newspaper. At the station, he got in line, paid his fare, and walked onto the train. As usual, he opened his newspaper to the financial page. Tyler was always interested in getting to the bottom line; at least that's what he thought was important. Every once in a while Tyler would look up from his paper. As his eyes scanned the train, he noticed other black-and-white newspapers with the faces of other travelers buried in them. Tyler was glad he worked for The Big Black and White Company. Why, with all this black and white around, he was sure to always have a job. But once in a while he felt a tug in his stomach. "Is this all there is?" he wondered.

Tyler was about to tuck his nose back into his paper to see if he could find any more details in the stock report when he noticed one face that wasn't buried in a newspaper.

"How odd," Tyler thought.

As he watched, Tyler noticed his fellow traveler's newspaper was crumpled on his lap and the man was actually gazing out the window! What was there to see on a typical gray day like this? As Tyler watched, he noticed the gentleman jotting something down on a small notepad.

"I wonder what that fellow does?" Tyler mused. "What kind of person can afford the time just to gaze out the window instead of keeping up with what's on the financial page?"

But Tyler didn't have a lot of time to wonder this morning. It was time for his stop, time to begin his day at The Big Black and White Company.

CHAPTER TWO

Tyler pulled on his black overcoat, got off the train, and walked several blocks to the entrance of The Big Black and White Company. He passed through the big iron gates and read the familiar slogan, which said:

> We are
> **THE BIG BLACK AND WHITE COMPANY**
> where everything is either
> **BLACK or WHITE**
> We maintain the time-honored tradition
> of doing things the way we
> have ALWAYS done them.

Tyler walked past security, showed them his black-and-white pass, rode up the elevator, and walked over to his desk. The sign on Tyler's desk read "Senior Idea Forager."

Tyler hung up his coat and straightened the papers on his desk. "Another day in the life of an idea forager," he thought as he sat down. "Maybe I'll find something new today."

Every day from nine to five, Tyler foraged for ideas for The Big Black and White Company. His job was to collect ideas that would make the black blacker and the white whiter. To find these ideas, he spent his days poring over the books and manuscripts of corporate history to see how his predecessors had done things. Sometimes he read the trade magazines, but he seldom found much information there. Mostly they extolled the virtues of The Big Black and White Company's very black, black and their very white, white. Information that did appear was usually information he already knew or that had been developed by his fellow workers at The Big Black and White Company. Besides, The Big Black and White Company published the magazines. It was all very believable, because if it's in black and white, you know it's true.

Sometimes during his day, Tyler would find a new idea. As soon as he had that one idea, he would write it on a black-and-white memo and schedule a time to see the idea ogre. Tyler wasn't sure what the idea ogre's title really was; he thought he was a vice president or at least someone very high up and trusted in the organization. But everyone in the company just called him the idea ogre. It seemed that the idea ogre didn't mind his "given" title. All Tyler knew was that this man's job was to see if the ideas Tyler found "fit" with the company's tradition of making the black blacker and white whiter.

When Tyler took an idea to the idea ogre, he would tell Tyler all the weaknesses in the idea; he'd look carefully at all the things wrong with it. That way, no ideas that might lead to dead ends or inappropriate use of company funds would be pursued in

The Big Black and White Company. The idea ogre had been with the company so many years that he knew which ideas would work and which would not. Besides, part of the idea ogre's job was to maintain the company's position: "We are The Big Black and White Company where everything is either black or white. We maintain the time-honored tradition of doing things the way we have always done them."

Today, before Tyler had a chance to forage for many ideas, the black phone on his gray desk rang. It was the idea ogre's secretary.

"Tyler, the idea ogre would like you to attend an important meeting in one hour in the large conference room. Will you be there?"

"Of course," Tyler replied. He always attended meetings that the idea ogre requested, even on such short notice.

"The large conference room?" Tyler thought. "Maybe, just maybe, the idea ogre has found one of my ideas fit to pursue and he has called a meeting to tell everyone about it. But then again, maybe someone else has come up with an idea."

Tyler wasn't sure whether he should be excited or worried about the meeting. Usually the idea ogre didn't tell his people what to expect. Tyler didn't have long to be concerned because the meeting time was quickly approaching.

CHAPTER THREE

Tyler walked down the tall black-and-white marble corridors to the executive conference room. He sat down in his usual place in a large black leather chair. As he gazed around the room, Tyler noticed several of the junior idea foragers there, along with the idea ogre and a couple of vice presidents. The vice president in charge of black manufacturing cleared his throat and started the meeting.

"Gentlemen, thank you so much for taking time out of your busy schedules to attend this meeting," his voice boomed through the white marble room and bounced off the black conference table.

"I have called you here today to let you know that another company has come onto the scene. Now we have seen many companies come and go in our business. Remember the cut-rate black and white company that began several years ago? You also might recall that white on white company that fizzled because of their lack of contrast. Well, I'm happy to report that we are still the world leader in our field. We have managed to crush all our competition because of our time-honored tradition of making the black blacker and the white whiter. However, a new company has come on the scene that I'd like you to be aware of. I'm sure we will continue to perform at our finest, even with this competition and will manage to crush them as we have crushed others in the past."

"What is this new company?" the vice president of white manufacturing asked.

"Well, my friends and associates," the vice president of black manufacturing chuckled, "this company is called...The Color Company. They don't sell just black and white; they sell color. It's called blue and green and purple and yellow and red."

"Too complicated!" the idea ogre scoffed. "Why, they won't know what colors to buy. It's too much choice."

"I don't think there is anything to worry about," the vice president of white manufacturing emphasized. "We will stand on the tried and true black and white. Why should people want colors anyway when black and white is good enough?"

"People won't be able to make decisions," one of the junior idea foragers chimed in. "Why, everyone knows that everything is either black or white."

"What do people need all those different shades and hues for anyway? Preposterous! It will just confuse them," the idea ogre exclaimed. "We need to decide for our customers what is good for them. Besides, it is too new, much too new and too outlandish to catch on."

"Well, it certainly hasn't been done like that in the past," Tyler interjected.

"It's just a fad!" the vice president for white manufacturing exclaimed. "Besides, what company can afford to make so many different colors?"

"Then we are agreed that we have absolutely nothing to worry about, gentlemen?" the vice president for black manufacturing asked.

"Absolutely nothing!" came the resounding cry from the other members in the room.

Tyler sat quietly for a moment and thought, "Color...Gee, I wonder...why didn't we think of that?"

After the meeting, Tyler went back to his desk and continued his search for ideas that would make the black blacker and the white whiter. And as the days and months went by, he continued to write one idea every day on the black-and-white memo and take it to the idea ogre. Once in a while the idea ogre would accept one of Tyler's ideas, but most of the time Tyler was told all the reasons why his ideas would not work.

Every day Tyler would ride back and forth on the train. Once in a while, when he would look up from his black-and-white newspaper and his bottom-lined reports, he would notice the rather odd traveler. Sometimes this fellow would read the black-and-white newspaper; at other times he would scribble a line or two on a piece of paper. And sometimes he just gazed out the window.

CHAPTER FOUR

ut they were wrong!

The customer wanted choice. The customer wanted more selection than just black or white. Soon customers began to buy more colors. They even bought more colors than they bought black and white. They bought all kinds of colors—blue and green and red and orange and yellow and purple and pink. As customers bought more and more colors, the sales of black and white plummeted. It seemed that colors were not just a novelty or a fad; they were also useful. Some of the colors even kept people safe. A red stop sign with white lettering showed up better at night than the usual black stop sign with white lettering. And mothers with babies like to dress their little girls in pink and their little boys in blue. Soon there were more and more colors. White barns suddenly turned red. Black-and-white photographs in books began to show shades of blue and green. Instead of black-and-white houses, people began painting houses with red and blue trim. Color was every-where.

As more and more color splashed on the scene, sales of black and white sank even further. The drop in sales began to hurt the bottom line. Tyler continued to propose ideas, and the idea ogre continued to find all the things wrong with them.

Then one day Tyler was called to the big conference room in The Big Black and White Company for a very important meeting. This time as he took his usual place at the black conference table, he noticed the president of The Big Black and White Company entering the room. Dressed in his finest black-and-white suit, the president took his place at the front of the conference table. He looked rather pale and white.

"Gentlemen," the president's voice rang sharply through the room. "I'm sure you're aware of the crisis in which this fine company finds itself. It seems that this new company, The Color Company, is threatening our market at a dangerous rate. You also may have noticed that things are not just black and white anymore. There is color out there!"

"Something must be done!" shouted the idea ogre. "We must find out what it is about color that is so appealing. We must find out how this company is able to come up with all those different shades."

Tyler noticed that the idea ogre was now chewing on a pink antacid tablet.

His face bright red, the idea ogre turned to Tyler.

"Tyler, you are the senior idea forager!" the idea ogre snapped. "You work from nine to five each day collecting ideas to make the black blacker and the white whiter. *You* find out why The Color Company is so successful!"

The rest of the room fell silent as all eyes turned to Tyler.

"Well, what are you going to do?" the idea ogre snarled.

Tyler replied meekly, "Using our time-honored approach of how things have been done before, I could search for reasons why they are successful. I could forage through magazines and books and find out what we have to say about them."

"No, no!" exclaimed the idea ogre.

"No, no!" exclaimed the vice president of white manufacturing.

"No, no!" exclaimed the vice president of black manufacturing.

"No, no!" exclaimed the president.

"This calls for strong measures!" the president warned. "Tyler, you must find another way to get those ideas."

Tyler was silent. The idea ogre was silent. The vice president of white manufacturing was silent. The vice president of black manufacturing was silent. Even the president of The Big Black and White Company was silent.

Very slowly and very quietly, Tyler stood up. "I'll get right on it, sirs," he said, his voice shaking. All the other managers in the room nodded.

CHAPTER FIVE

"How can I find out about The Color Company?" Tyler asked himself.

Finally, after dismissing a couple of ideas, Tyler decided to try the direct approach. After all, that is the way you get to the bottom line.

Tyler looked up the number of The Color Company in the yellow pages. Their ad was in red and blue.

"Oh no," Tyler groaned. "It's worse than we thought—even the phone company is going color."

Tyler picked up the receiver of his black phone, dialed the main number of The Color Company, and asked to speak to someone in the color department. He was surprised at how pleasant everyone sounded on the phone and how helpful they were, even after he told them he was from The Big Black and White Company.

After a few rings on the color department extension, a friendly voice answered.

"This is the color director. May I help you?"

Tyler swallowed hard. "Will this person talk to me?" he wondered. "After all, I am the competition."

"This is Tyler, senior idea forager for The Big Black and White Company."

"Oh yes," the color director replied, "I thought I might be hearing from you folks soon. How can I help you?"

"Well, I...I..." Tyler felt his throat tighten. "I was wondering if I could come and talk to you about your company?"

"Of course. I'll be happy to talk with you. I'll be out of town for several days soon, so if it's convenient for you, why don't we meet first thing tomorrow morning?"

"Tomorrow morning is fine," Tyler replied.

"You realize that some things are confidential, like how we mix our colors, but I'd be happy to tell you how we do our business here. You say you are the senior idea forager?" the color director asked.

"Why yes," Tyler replied.

"Well, I'm sure you'll be interested in the way we deal with ideas around here. Until tomorrow then?"

"Yes, tomorrow at nine o'clock?"

"That will be fine," the color director replied.

Tyler hung up the phone. He felt a little dazed. "He's willing to see me first thing tomorrow? Wow, that's service!"

CHAPTER SIX

The next morning Tyler stayed on the train three stops past his usual stop. As Tyler stood up to get off the train, the fellow who scribbled notes and looked out the window got off the train with him. Tyler made his way to The Color Company and noticed that his fellow passenger was also headed that direction. As Tyler stopped at security to get his blue-and-silver visitors' pass, the "train scribbler," as Tyler called him, flashed his pass, nodded in greeting to the security guard, and walked quickly into the building. For the first time Tyler noticed how nicely dressed this gentleman was. He was wearing color: a light blue shirt, a blue jacket, and red tie.

As Tyler was escorted up the elevator to the color department, he noticed all the different shades and hues of colors. There was dark blue carpet and light pink marble walls. Small green trees with dark brown trunks stood in orangish-red pots. Tyler found himself smiling. "Those colors are nice," he thought. "They kind of put a different light on the world."

Tyler noticed something else different about this company. Everyone seemed interested in their work and involved in what they were doing. It wasn't quiet and subdued as it was in the halls of The Big Black and White Company. The building teemed with energy and excitement. Tyler even heard people laughing. Everywhere Tyler looked he saw people talking, drawing on chart paper, working in small groups, and jotting notes on cards and pieces of paper. And there was color, vibrant color everywhere.

Tyler's security escort introduced him to the secretary in the color director's office. The color director's secretary seemed pleasant and impressed with Tyler's background.

"Oh, so you're from The Big Black and White Company," she said. "I buy all of your newspapers. They always have so much detail. I trust what your papers have to say. After all, it is in black and white."

Tyler smiled and sat down.

"The color director will be with you in a moment."

As she left the office, Tyler noticed the secretary was wearing a red blouse with a blue skirt.

"Color...hmmm..."

Just then the color director strode into the room. He put his hand out to shake Tyler's hand. Tyler tried to smile but gulped instead. It was he! It was the fellow on the train. It was the train scribbler!

"It's you!" Tyler exclaimed. "I mean, we ride the same train."

"The same train?" the color director asked. "Oh yes, I think I've seen you a time or two on the train. You always get off a couple of stops before I do. Of course, that would be the stop for The Big Black and White Company."

"To be honest," Tyler tried to explain, "the reason I noticed you is because you aren't always reading the black-and-white paper on the train. Frankly, I've noticed that you sometimes look out the window and even write on pieces of paper."

"Gee, I didn't realize I was that different," the color director said with a smile. "I suppose I'll have to watch my train behavior in the future."

"Oh no. I didn't mean it that way."

"Great start," Tyler thought. "Insult the guy before you get to know him."

The color director smiled gently. "Tyler, do you know what I do on the train?"

"No, what?"

"I think. Sometimes I even create on the train."

Tyler turned white. "Create on the train? Create in the midst of all that noise and confusion? Don't you have to be in a special place to create? I must be at my desk at The Big Black and White Company between the hours of nine and five to get ideas."

"I am in a special place," the color director replied. "Although the train is a busy place, there aren't any phones ringing or people wanting to talk to me. So I have a little time to be alone and to think. The special place is what you create in your mind, not necessarily in what surrounds you. In fact," the color director smiled, "we find that some of the best ideas we get are when we aren't looking for them. Sometimes our people get their ideas in the shower, while driving a car, or even falling asleep at night. We've given each of them an idea trap so they can catch their ideas whenever and wherever they come to them. In fact, Tyler, we don't have a position for an idea forager like you at The Color Company. Instead, you might say that everyone here is an idea forager."

Creativity Rule 1

Capture ideas whenever and wherever they come to you. Many of our best ideas are "free," often coming to us when we're relaxed and not consciously working on a problem. Record your ideas immediately.

Tyler was shocked, "You mean everyone in your company is an idea forager?"

"Yes, Tyler, everyone, absolutely everyone—from the people who design the colors to the people who clean up after the color mixers. Nobody knows how to do a job better than the people doing that job. Those people are the ones who create the ideas, or 'forage' them in your company's words. They are the people who evaluate the ideas, and they are the ones who implement them."

"But what about the idea ogre?" Tyler blurted.

"Idea ogre?" the color director asked slowly. "What's that?"

"Well," Tyler felt his face turning red, "he's not really the idea ogre. He's a vice president. He's the person who evaluates all the ideas that I forage for. He decides whether the idea is good or bad and if we should do anything with it at The Big Black and White Company."

"Tyler, we don't have an idea ogre," the color director replied. "The people who do the jobs evaluate their own ideas. They improve the ideas, and they put them to work."

Tyler gulped. "No idea foragers? No idea ogre?"

"You might say, Tyler, that we've tried to create a place where people can feel good about being creative. We've tried to create an environment for being creative."

"An environment for being creative?" Tyler looked around the room. "Why, I don't see any great paintings or hear profound works of music playing or even smell incense burning."

The color director smiled, "Tyler, you don't need all those trappings to be creative. The environment for being creative is the way we treat each other in this company...the way we respect each other's ideas. We try to be open to possibilities that people come up with. That's why we have so many different colors. We've found that it's not only what you say about someone's idea but *how* you say it that makes the difference. We've found that our body expressions, our gestures, and our tone of voice many times indicate more about what we think of another person's idea than the words we use. So we are very careful when someone comes up with a new idea; even in The Color Company we have to watch the way we treat those fledgling ideas. Part of the way we nurture new ideas is how we talk about them."

"Everybody an idea forager? No idea ogre? Verbal and nonverbal

---

Creativity Rule 2

Model openness and acceptance of ideas. **Watch your verbal and nonverbal communication**. Much of our response to others' ideas is communicated nonverbally.

communication? Climate for creativity? Wow! There is such a difference here! Frankly I'm a little overwhelmed," Tyler sighed.

The color director nodded.

"You use the word *creativity* so much around here. Isn't creativity something that geniuses have?" Tyler asked. "You see, even though I am the senior idea forager, I'm really not creative. I've never painted a painting or written a beautiful piece of music or even cooked a gourmet meal. I consider myself a pretty ordinary guy. I just forage and collect ideas. I'm not one of those crazy creative types."

"You don't have to be an artist or a musician to be creative, and you certainly don't have to be crazy," the color director explained. "Here at The Color Company, we believe that everyone is creative. Everyone, from the paint designers to the people who clean the floors, has ideas that could make us all much more successful."

"Part of being creative is an attitude. It's an attitude of looking at problems as opportunities. Another part of being creative is asking why?"

The color director spoke with a rush of excitement. "Another part is developing some habits for being creative, and yet another part is realizing that we are all creative and that creativity can be developed like any other skill."

Tyler sat back in his chair. "Wow! This is almost too much. I think I'm on overload."

"Want to take a little break?"

"Please," Tyler sighed.

CHAPTER SEVEN

W ould you like another cup of coffee, Tyler?"

"That would be great, thanks. By the way, how did you get the idea of color?" Tyler asked.

"Well, we stretched beyond the obvious. Your company made black and white. So we asked ourselves, what other colors might there be?"

"Other colors?" Tyler asked. "Why, we never thought of asking if there were such things as other colors. We just concentrated on making the black blacker and the white whiter. By the way, what is this stretching beyond the obvious?"

"That's one of those creativity techniques that I mentioned; that's one of the ways we get new ideas."

"You mean, you don't go out and forage for them?"

"Well, we do forage for ideas. As I said, everyone is an idea forager, but that's just *one* way to get new ideas. Here at The Color Company we have lots of ways to get new ideas.

"One of the ways is that we ask ourselves questions, like 'Why?' Why just black and white? What if there was something else? We redefined the problem. We looked at this situation in a lot of different ways. We realized that we probably couldn't do a very good job of making the black blacker and the white whiter. Your company was already doing an excellent job of that. So we tried a different angle. We tried a different approach to the whole area of consumer colors. It took us awhile to settle on the direction we needed to go. We asked ourselves many times, 'Why this approach?'" The color director leaned back in his chair. "We ran into dead ends, had some frustrations, and made a lot of mistakes, but finally the whole color concept emerged. When we looked at the problem from a fresh perspective, we realized this was the right approach to take."

"Mistakes?" Tyler asked. "You admit that you make mistakes?"

"Oh yes, lots of them," the color director replied. "We actually learn from our mistakes. Tell me, Tyler. How does The Big Black and White Company deal with mistakes?"

Creativity Rule 3

Redefine your problem in many ways. Ask yourself "Why?" Many times we set out to solve the wrong problem. Challenge your assumptions.

"Well, it certainly is different at The Big Black and White Company. There it's important to work really hard and not to make any mistakes." Tyler straightened his black tie. "That's why I report to the idea ogre. His job is to ensure we don't make any mistakes. We have to make the black blacker and the white whiter...without mistakes. We have to get it right the first time...all the time."

"I see," the color director replied. "Well, we've found there are two ways to look at failure—as something that should never happen, or as something we can learn from. Everybody makes mistakes, and we believe that successful employees and successful companies look at mistakes as learning experiences. We ask ourselves, What can we learn from this mistake? Sometimes we've found that a mistake in one area may be a success in another. A color we were trying to create for stop signs really works well for houses. As a matter of fact, Tyler," the color director continued, "we've learned that there is a method to our mistake-making. If we take the time to consciously go outside the problem area, we can create new connections that can lead to solutions for other problems."

"Go outside the problem area?" Tyler looked puzzled. "How do you do that?"

"Maybe I can give you an example. A couple of years ago when we started the company, we were trying to make a color that people could see in the dark." The color director walked to the window and pointed toward the parking lot. "We knew that one of the best markets would be the stop-sign market. There were lots of stop signs, and people were having automobile accidents because they couldn't see the black-and-white signs at night. We experimented with all sorts of colors—greens and reds and yellows and blues. But nothing seemed to work. You still couldn't see the sign at night. Then one day we were meeting with one of our suppliers—the one who sells us the cleaner for our color-mixing machines. We use so much pigment in our colors that the cleaner has to be very strong to thoroughly clean the mixing tanks. This fellow was showing us all the virtues of his product.

He wanted us to see how well his chemical cleaned the vats so he turned off the lights in the color-mixing room and shined a flashlight into one of the stainless steel vats he had cleaned. We noticed that his product cleaned the vat pretty well, but we also saw a strange glow in the vat. Something in his vat cleaner glowed when the light hit it. When we analyzed his cleaner, we were able to isolate the chemical that caused the glow. We then mixed the proper proportion of that chemical with our red stop sign paint, and eureka!—a stop-sign that glowed in the dark. Well, actually it was a stop sign that glowed when car lights hit it."

"That's a nice story. But I'm still not sure I see the point." Tyler looked puzzled.

"The point is, Tyler, we were looking for a way to clean color vats more effectively, but we found our stop-sign paint. That's a pretty big stretch, from vat cleaner to a stop sign that glows in the dark. That's what I mean by going outside of the problem area and looking for connections from other worlds."

Tyler nodded with understanding.

"Now we regularly ask ourselves the question: 'What ideas can I get for solving this problem from a completely different world?' As a matter of fact, we have found this question so effective that we make a habit of asking it when we get stuck on a problem."

Creativity Rule 4

Go outside of the problem area. Look for connections from other areas for solving problems. Ask yourself, "What ideas can I get for solving this problem from a completely different world?"

CHAPTER EIGHT

So, Tyler, it's been quite a morning. How are you doing?"

"Frankly, I haven't done this much thinking in years. There is just so much to understand, and there are so many exciting ways to solve problems."

"Are you hungry?" the color director asked as he looked at his watch.

"Why, yes I am. I really hadn't thought about it, but now that you mention it, I'm starved."

"Yes, this creativity work does have a way of giving you an appetite. Let's continue our discussion over lunch. The cafeteria will be a good place to explore some other creativity methods."

"The cafeteria?" Tyler asked. "You mean someone in your high position doesn't go to the executive dining room?"

The color director smiled, "Sorry, Tyler, no executive dining room here. All of us, from the president of The Color Company to the color mixers eat lunch in the cafeteria. We believe it's important for everyone who works at The Color Company at least to see each other. Of course we do have a small dining room for private meetings now and then, but most of the time everyone eats together in the cafeteria. If people need to talk to the president for a moment, and he is available, they can approach him after lunch."

Tyler was impressed. "Wow, that's amazing! We hardly ever see the people who run The Big Black and White Company. They have so many executive dining rooms that you could get lost in them. Many of the people in our company haven't even met the president. All they know is that a big black car drives up early in the morning, parks in the president's spot, and then leaves late at night. To see him in the company cafeteria would be a shock."

"Well, Tyler, let me take you to lunch in our cafeteria. Who knows, you might even get to meet our president."

Tyler followed the color director down the hall and into the elevator. Again he noticed all the activity around the building and all the color. Color was everywhere.

Tyler and the color director picked up their green trays and walked through the cafeteria line. All around the room Tyler saw people talking excitedly in small groups. Sometimes a group would break into loud laughter, or someone would scribble on one of the paper napkins. Everyone was dressed in different colors—reds and blues and greens and purples. Tyler and the color director found a quiet place in the cafeteria and sat down.

"Tyler, what hand do you eat with?" the color director asked.

"My right hand," Tyler replied, reaching for his salad fork.

"OK, then I'd like you to try something."

"What's that?" Tyler asked.

"I'd like you to try eating your salad with your left hand instead of your right."

Tyler looked at the color director, shrugged his shoulders, and switched his fork to his left hand. He stabbed at a piece of lettuce and knocked a tomato out of his salad bowl.

"I never did like tomatoes," Tyler chuckled at the color director.

The color director smiled back.

"Does it feel a little uncomfortable, Tyler?"

"Yes, of course it does. I'm not used to eating with my left hand."

"OK, Tyler, then let's try this. Put your fork down and cross your arms across your chest."

The color director leaned back and crossed his arms across his chest. Tyler did the same.

"Now, Tyler, which arm is on top?"

"My left arm."

"Good, now I want you to uncross your arms and then recross them with the other arm on the top."

Tyler uncrossed his arms and tried to recross them, this time with his right arm on the top.

"I feel like a pretzel," Tyler said, squirming. "I can hardly cross my arms this way, and if I do, it's very uncomfortable."

"I know what you mean. Even though I do this little exercise with people here in the company a lot, I still get very uncomfortable if I try to switch my arms. But something is going on here other than the hands we eat with and the way we cross our arms."

"Habits!" Tyler shouted. "I have a habit of eating with my right hand and crossing my arms with my left arm on top. That's the way I've always done it."

"Exactly!" the color director replied. "And doing things the way we have always done them can be very comfortable, but it can be dangerous. Our world doesn't stay the same, and if we continue to do things as we have done them in the past, we can be left behind. Now, Tyler, don't get me wrong. I'm not saying that all habits are bad. I have the habit of driving my car on the right side of the road and stopping at red lights, and I get pretty upset when anyone gets 'creative' with me on that."

Tyler laughed as the color director continued. "But what tends to happen is that our habitual ways of thinking get in the way when we want to create new ideas. Some of us even have the habit of taking the first idea we come up with and running with it—even if we run right off the edge of a cliff."

"So how do you get over a habit that isn't helpful?"

"Glad you asked that," the color director replied as he put down his cup of coffee. "We have found the best way to deal with a habit that is not productive is to replace it with another habit. So we have developed some creativity habits here.

"When we find ourselves stuck on a problem, we ask ourselves a few questions. Questions like...'How else can I do this?' 'What if...?' and 'How can I use something that doesn't fit with this at all?' Remember that story of the paint-cleaning compound and the stop-sign paint?"

Tyler nodded as he chewed his sandwich.

"That's where we got the creativity habit of using something that doesn't fit with the problem at all."

"You know, Mr. Color Director," Tyler began as he put his napkin on his plate, "all of this stuff is really great, but I just can't get my hands around it. Are there more concrete methods I can use to improve my creativity? Are there some bottom-line creativity methods that my company would understand? Aren't there basic tools I can use to solve problems consistently time after time?"

> ## Creativity Rule 5
> **Develop creativity habits.** When working on a challenge or an opportunity, ask yourself: "How else can I do this?" "What if...?" "How can I use something that doesn't fit with this at all?"

"As a matter of fact, Tyler, there are. Let's go back up to my office. I've got a few things I want to show you."

CHAPTER NINE

S o, Tyler, how many ideas do you get on a good day of idea foraging?" the color director asked as he sat down next to his desk.

Tyler took a seat across from the color director. "Oh, usually one or two," he replied.

"Hmmm, I see," the color director mused. "Why do you only get one or two?"

"Because I'm only looking for the *good* ideas—the ideas that I know will make the black blacker and the white whiter."

"And what do you do with those ides, if I may ask?"

"Well, I write them up on a black-and-white idea memo and take them to the idea ogre—uh, the vice president. His job is to find all the things that are wrong with the idea so we don't pursue a bad idea. He looks for all the reasons the idea won't work."

"I see," said the color director. "Would you like to get a lot more ideas so you can increase your chances of getting a good one?"

"Absolutely!" Tyler exclaimed.

"OK, one way you can immediately increase your idea productivity is to separate your imaginative thinking from your judgmental thinking."

"What do you mean?" Tyler asked.

"Don't judge your ideas while you are trying to come up with them," the color director emphasized.

Tyler looked puzzled.

"Now, Tyler, I know that all of your life you have been taught that as soon as you come up with an idea you immediately need to judge whether it is right or wrong. We were all taught that way. But when you are foraging for creative ideas, it's important to separate your imaginative thinking from your judgmental thinking."

The color director leaned forward in his chair, "Tyler, do you drive your car with one foot on the gas and the other on the brake at the same time?"

"Of course not. That would ruin the car, and even if it didn't, I wouldn't get very far."

"My point exactly," said the color director, nodding his head. "And that is precisely what you are doing when you try to generate ideas and evaluate them at the same time. You ruin the fun in the creative process, and you usually don't get ideas that are very interesting. So just as you don't drive a car with one foot on the gas and one on the brake, it's important to separate your imaginative thinking from your judgmental thinking. You need to suspend your judgment while you are generating ideas."

"Oh," Tyler replied, "that sounds easy. Just come up with a couple of ideas and then look at what's wrong with them. That way I can eliminate all the bad ideas and keep the good ones."

"No, that's not quite it, Tyler. First, we've found there is no such thing as a 'bad' idea. All ideas have some positive aspects...and some not-so-positive ele-

> ## Creativity Rule 6
> **Separate your imaginative thinking from your judgmental thinking.** When generating ideas, don't criticize your own ideas or the ideas of others. After you have generated a number of ideas, then evaluate them, but don't try to generate and evaluate at the same time.

ments. The key is to build on the positive elements to make the idea stronger. We try not to weaken the idea with criticism."

"But how do you do that?" Tyler asked. "My boss always tells me what's wrong with the ideas I collect. That way, he says, we won't waste time with stupid ideas that everybody knows won't work."

"Hmmm, I see," snorted the color director. "Come over here a minute, Tyler." The color director walked over to the blackboard in his office and picked up a piece of white chalk.

The color director looked at Tyler and smiled, "Tyler, this chalk and blackboard are among the few things around this place that *are* either black or white."

"I guess you're right," Tyler replied as his eyes scanned the color director's office.

On the blackboard the color director sketched a design that he called a 'wheelbarrow.'

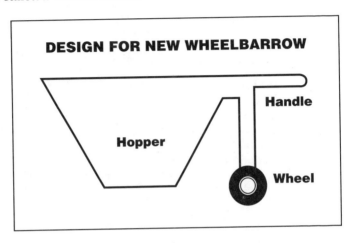

DESIGN FOR NEW WHEELBARROW

Handle

Hopper

Wheel

Underneath the wheelbarrow, he wrote the word "Comments."

"Now, Tyler, give me your comments on this deign," the color director said.

Tyler scratched his head for a moment and replied, "I'm sorry, but, well, the wheel is in the wrong place, and the handle is too short. The hopper is too big, and it will tip over when you try to fill it. And it looks like it's backward, and who would buy a wheelbarrow like this anyway? Is this even a wheelbarrow?"

The color director grinned and made some marks on his paper as Tyler commented on the design.

"Now, Tyler, what would you say if I told you that this wheelbarrow really exists, and that it really is in use?"

"Oh, come on...really?"

"Yes, Tyler, it really is used. You see, it's used for high-rise construction. To operate this wheelbarrow you push down on the handle instead of pulling up on it. Because you push down on it, the wheelbarrow has a lower center of gravity and it's much easier to control. Now that's pretty important if you're thirty-eight stories above the ground on a steel girder with only a safety net below you. It's used to haul those big bolts that construction workers use to hold buildings together."

"OK, but what does that have to do with getting new ideas?"

"Tyler, I asked you for comments, and what did I jot down on my sheet of paper?"

The color director handed Tyler the pad.

"Why, everything I told you was a criticism. It was a negative comment on the wheelbarrow."

"Right, Tyler. That's what new ideas look like sometimes. They can look pretty strange. But there is an even more important process here. What would have happened if I had redrawn the wheelbarrow according to your comments?"

"You'd have the same old wheelbarrow with the one wheel in the front and the two long handles in the back. And you would probably have a lot of construction workers who lost their balance and fell off buildings."

"Exactly," said the color director with a nod. He returned to his desk chair as he continued. "What we have found, even in our company, is that many times the immediate reaction to a new idea is to kill it. That's why we have a special method for evaluating ideas."

"Sounds interesting. What is it?" asked Tyler as he pulled his chair closer to the color director's desk.

"Around here, we evaluate new ideas by first looking at the pluses of an idea—its strengths. We analyze what is good about an idea before we tear it down. We try to come up with at least three pluses, three specific things that are good about the idea we are considering.

Next, we look at the potential in the new idea. These potentials might be future gains or spin-offs of the idea. For example, a color we develop for cars might also be good for submarines or airplanes or for an entirely different market than we originally intended.

Finally, we realize that no idea is perfect. So the last aspect of evaluating ideas is to discuss our concerns. But we word the concerns, or the downsides of the idea, in a special way. We phrase the concerns as we would phrase a problem statement."

"Word the concerns like a problem statement? What do you mean?" Tyler asked.

"Let's say an idea will be costly to develop. Instead of saying that the idea is too expensive or that we can't afford it, we phrase the concerns like, 'How might we reduce the cost' or 'How might we raise money for the project?' Does that make sense?"

"Hmmm...yes it does."

"Good, then let's try it. Let's look at the pluses, potentials, and concerns of the wheelbarrow." The color director walked over to the chalkboard and pointed to the drawing.

"What do you like about this design, Tyler?"

Tyler got out of his chair and stood a few feet away from the board.

"Well, the hopper is big so it would hold a lot."

"Good, that's one. What else do you like about the wheelbarrow?"

"The design looks pretty simple, so it would probably be relatively easy to manufacture."

"OK, that's two. How about one more?"

Tyler studied the drawing. "OK, hmmm...well, with the wheel in the back, it would be easy to dump cargo out of the front of the wheelbarrow."

"Great, Tyler. Now let's take a look at the potentials of the wheelbarrow. What potential or possible future gains do you see in this design?"

"Well," said Tyler as he scratched his head, "the handle is pretty short, so we could probably save money on handle material."

"Good, two more."

Tyler pointed to the design. "Because the wheel is in the back of the wheelbarrow, you don't have to lift it. Maybe people with less strength could use this wheelbarrow more easily than the traditional one."

"That's it, Tyler. One more."

"Hmmm, if there is a market for this wheelbarrow and we manufacture it first, we could beat all the competition and make a killing on this new design."

"Terrific, you're getting the idea!" the color director exclaimed. "Now, what concerns do you have about this design?"

"Will it work?" Tyler replied quickly.

"OK, Tyler, let's see if we can make that concern a little more specific. Does your concern relate to the design?"

"Yes it does."

"Then let's concentrate on the design. And remember, phrase your concern as you would phrase a problem statement."

"OK, how's this? How might we pretest the design?"

"Good, Tyler." The color director encouraged him with a nod. "Any other concerns?"

"Yes...the market."

"How about a problem statement?"

"Uhm...how might we determine if there is a market for this design?"

"Nice."

"You know, I've got a couple of ideas how we could market test this idea. We could build a prototype and then take it out to..."

"You see, you're doing it!" the color director shouted.

"Doing what?" asked Tyler a bit shocked.

"As soon as you phrased your concerns about the idea like problem statements, your mind immediately started creating ideas for solving that problem. That's the beauty of the Pluses, Potentials, and Concerns technique. We call it the PPC for short."

A smile quickly appeared on Tyler's face. "You know, this is great. I'm beginning to see how this could really work in my company. If the idea ogre evaluated my ideas this way, I'd feel challenged to find a way to overcome the concerns. Right now, all he does is tell me what is wrong, and the idea dies right there on the floor of his office. Maybe I ought to call him the idea executioner. He kills more ideas than he lets survive."

"Now, not so fast" the color director interjected. "The idea ogre probably doesn't know any better. He thinks he's doing the right thing by criticizing your ideas. He certainly doesn't want to waste The Big Black and White Company's money on a worthless idea, and he has never been taught to look first at the strengths of the idea and then consider the weaknesses. Many people don't know about these creativity tools. No idea is perfect; every idea has its weaknesses. We have found that the PPC approach enables us to overcome the weaknesses in the idea instead of letting it die. That's why we have so many color selections, and we are getting more."

"You know, I really like that approach. I don't feel like my idea is dumb when you evaluate it that way."

"That's exactly what we have found. Our people may bring us ideas that aren't feasible to develop at the time, and if we tell them their idea is stupid, we may not ever get another idea from that person. By using this format our people at least have a chance to explore the idea, refine it, and possibly develop a new approach. We never want to discourage them from sharing their ideas with us. Our employees have so much to teach us."

Creativity Rule 7

Evaluate ideas by considering the Pluses or strengths of the idea first; then list the Potentials in the idea; then list the Concerns (PPC). When you determine your concerns about an idea, phrase your concerns as you would phrase a question or problem statement. This way your mind will immediately begin to look for ways to overcome the concerns instead of disregarding the entire idea.

Chapter Ten

I really like that PPC technique, Mr. Color Director. It gives me some concrete ways to evaluate my ideas. You know, I bet if I came into the idea ogre's office with the pluses, potentials, and concerns of my ideas outlined, and ideas for overcoming those concerns, I might get him to approve more of my ideas."

"Yes, you probably would increase the number of ideas you got approved. When our people come to us with their ideas outlined in that form, we know they've thought about each idea and have anticipated some of the concerns. If they really want to get the idea implemented, they usually have ten or twelve ways to overcome each of the concerns they've identified. Our people treat this as a challenge. They try to anticipate all the objections upper management might raise. Then, when we bring up concerns about the idea, they already have ways to solve them. Most of the time, after smoothing out a few rough edges on the idea, we have birthed a new concept."

"That really helps. Thanks. Now at least I have a way to evaluate my ideas. But how many ideas do I have to come up with to get a good one?" Tyler asked. "Do I have to come up with hundreds of ideas to get a breakthrough? I don't have the time for that."

"No, you don't. But we've found it very helpful to set a quota or an idea goal. On some of our problems we've found that thirty to forty ideas is a good goal. In our idea sessions, with problems that are pretty well defined, we find that the first eight to ten ideas are the usual ways for solving the problem. Between idea ten and twenty our ideas tend to get a little more ridiculous. But those ridiculous or wild ideas are very important because they help form the sophisticated combinations that usually occur around idea thirty-five to forty."

"OK, so I set a quota of forty ideas and then stop when I reach that quota."

"Whoa! Let's not be so rigid here."

"Hmmm...it must be all my years with The Big Black and White Company coming through."

The color director and Tyler both laughed.

"Tyler, if you hit the idea quota and you find yourself really moving, don't stop. Let yourself go. You will be very pleased with the ideas you get. We've found that after an individual or a creativity team has reached their idea

---

Creativity Rule 8

When working to solve a problem, **set a quota of at least forty ideas**. To get new ideas, it is important to stretch beyond the obvious ways for solving a problem. The more ways you have of accomplishing your goal, the greater are your chances of doing it.

goal they experience a psychological freedom. Many of the ideas they get after that quota are really terrific."

"Great, now I've got the formula. Now I know how to be creative. I separate my imagination from judgment, I come up with forty ideas, and I evaluate my most promising ideas with a PPC." Tyler smiled broadly.

"Not so fast," the color director interrupted. It's going to take practice, just as any skill takes practice.

"Tyler, I think you are beginning to realize that everyone is creative and that there is nothing mysterious about being creative. Creativity is just a way of dealing with the information about our world that we take in every day. When you first use these techniques, it may seem awkward, even contrived. The first few times a person throws a baseball, plays the piano, or does a PPC on an idea, it feels strange. So you need to practice. Every day you need to practice being creative, using the creativity habits we talked about earlier."

Creativity Rule 9

We are all creative, but realize that **creativity requires practice** and development as any other skill does.

CHAPTER ELEVEN

T hank you for sharing your time with me. This was a terrific day." Tyler sat back in his chair and smiled at the color director as he sipped a cold drink.

"You're welcome. I really enjoy talking about this creativity 'stuff.' I find it exciting to share these things with other people like you."

Suddenly Tyler straightened up in his chair. "Oh no, I've got a problem here."

"A problem? What do you mean?"

"Well, I've been enjoying myself so much today and learning so many things, but now I have to find a way to take this back to my company," Tyler sputtered.

"Yes," the color director nodded slowly.

"But, but...how? Your company and my company are so different. It's like being in two different worlds. How will they ever understand these methods? They're so locked into their perspective that everything is either black or white."

"Hmmm...I see what you mean. Well, I know I've been giving you lots of answers today, but I'm not sure what to tell you about that question. You're the one who lives in that organization, and you probably know more about how you can get these methods into The Big Black and White Company than I do."

"Yes...but I'm different now, and everybody else has had a usual day at The Big Black and White Company. You know, making the black blacker and the white whiter."

"Right, Tyler. I suppose the only advice I can give you is to adopt an attitude that we have around here. We believe that every problem has something to teach us and there is no such thing as a problem without a gift. Some of the biggest problems we have had in The Color Company have taught us the greatest lessons. So now, when we have a 'problem,' we refocus that concept of a 'problem' and look at it as an opportunity. Like mistakes, we look at problems as opportunities for learning."

"You're saying I have an opportunity to get these creativity methods into The Big Black and White Company?"

"Yes, Tyler," the color director replied, "probably one of the greatest opportunities you will have in your lifetime, because you can change your company. You can begin to make some changes in those stale, time-honored traditions that aren't effective anymore. And besides, your company sent you here to find out

---

Creativity Rule 10

Look at problems as opportunities. Every problem we encounter has something to teach us. As Richard Bach, author of *Illusions*, said, "There is no such thing as a problem without a gift for you in its hand. We seek problems because we need their gifts."

---

why we are so successful. They're ready for change."

"Thank you, Mr. Color Director. I guess I can make a difference...but, but, I'm just one person and The Big Black and White Company is a huge organization."

"That's right. But just as every cell in your body makes a difference in your well-being, every person in your company makes a difference in the company's well-being. It doesn't matter how small you think you are. If one cell changes, the cells around it begin to change, and soon more cells change, and eventually the whole system begins to change. If disease works that way, being healthy can also work that way."

"I suppose you are right. It certainly is worth a try."

Tyler stood up and shook the color director's hand.

"Let me walk you down."

"Thanks, I'd appreciate that."

On his way out of the building, Tyler again noticed all the color and the activity. He noticed the blue carpet, the green wall tiles, and the red blossoms on the plants in orange-brown clay pots.

"It really is magnificent—" he thought to himself, "All this life and all this color."

"See you on the train tomorrow morning?" the color director asked.

"Yes, until then."

CHAPTER TWELVE

Tyler didn't go back to work that afternoon. He needed time to think. He rode the train home in silence. He bought his usual black-and-white newspaper, read a few pages, and then put it down. Soon he found himself gazing out the window. When he realized what he was doing, he looked around the train to see if anyone had noticed.

"I hope no one else saw me looking out the window and not studying the paper," he thought.

"Wait a minute," came a voice from inside of him. "You don't always have to read the paper. You could get an idea or two on the train."

"I'm beginning to sound like the color director," he thought. "Maybe I could forage for ideas without being at my desk in my office from nine to five," came another thought.

As Tyler got off the train and began to walk toward his house, he suddenly stopped.

"Wait a minute. How else could I do this?" he asked himself. "I think I'll take a different way home today. Maybe I'll find something new, or maybe I'll get a fresh perspective on my neighborhood."

As Tyler walked home, he noticed more and more houses painted all sorts of colors.

"More color," he thought. "It's everywhere!"

The next morning when Tyler got up. He washed his face with white soap and brushed his teeth with white toothpaste. He pulled on his black socks, buckled the belt to his gray pants, tied his black shoes, buttoned his white shirt, tied his black tie, and slipped into his gray jacket.

He wandered into his kitchen and sat down for breakfast. But this morning instead of having gray oatmeal, black coffee, and white toast, he looked through his cupboard for something different.

"What about some fruit or some cheese or even some cold pizza from last night?" he thought. And as Tyler ate his breakfast, he tried, for a couple of moments, to eat with his left hand.

"It still feels funny," he thought, "but it sure is interesting to try a new way."

That morning as Tyler rode the train to work, he sat and talked with the color director. After a while both of them fell silent and took time to think. The color director thought about new colors, and Tyler thought about how he would explain to the people in his company what he had learned the day before.

Soon, Tyler stood up to get off the train.

"I learned a lot yesterday," he said, smiling.

"Thanks. Good luck at your company today," the color director responded.

"I'm gonna need it. See you."

Tyler walked the few blocks to the entrance of The Big Black and White Company. He passed the familiar slogan.

We are
THE BIG BLACK AND WHITE COMPANY
where everything is either
BLACK or WHITE
We maintain the time-honored tradition
of doing things the way we
have ALWAYS done them.

Tyler chuckled and shook his head. "I have my work cut out for me today."

He walked into his office, took off his overcoat, and sat down at his desk. He got out some paper and began to outline a report for his meeting with the president and the vice presidents of black and white manufacturing. They'd be anxious to know what he had discovered about why The Color Company was so successful.

Tyler's head was swimming with all he had learned the day before.

"I learned that it's the way they look at problems and treat each other's ideas in that company that makes them so successful. But how can we make that happen here?"

He stared at the white walls as he looked over his black desk.

"Do something new," came a small voice from inside him. "That's what they'd do at The Color Company."

"But what can I do?"

Suddenly something clicked.

"Wait a minute, I don't have to be at my desk from nine to five to get ideas. I need a fresh approach."

Tyler stood up. He stuffed a pen and a pad of paper into his shirt pocket, threw on his overcoat, and opened his office door.

He smiled broadly at his secretary. "I'm taking a walk."

The secretary stared at Tyler with her mouth open.

"Good idea," he thought. "Why didn't I think of that—Wait a minute. I did!"

The Beginning...

Epilogue

Nice story you say? But do those ten rules for becoming more creative really work? Can I use them on a day-to-day basis? Can I achieve extraordinary results with creativity? The resounding answer to each question is yes! Look at how creativity methods are being applied in business, education, and human services.

Our company, Innovation Resources, Inc., has seen firsthand what happens when we help organizations implement these principles.

To create a culture that fosters teamwork and innovation, employees at Mazda Motor Manufacturing, USA were trained in creative problem solving, team building, and continuous improvement. The result: Employees met productivity and quality levels, not minutes but *days ahead of schedule*. In fact, supervisors report that employees trained in creativity came up to speed two *weeks* faster than untrained counterparts!

When first asked by a key customer to supply paper that was 95 percent bright, Mead Paper said, "We simply can't do it." In fact, Mead struggled for years to enhance the brightness of its papers without success. Invigorated by a creativity workshop, however, Mead assembled a team to tackle the problem. The result: The team improved the brightness of Mead's paper, developed a new *world-class* line of products superior to any of Mead's competitors, and came up with a new process that saves more than $500,000 per year!

When Janet DiClaudio, director of medical records, joined Candler Hospital, three hundred records were backlogged, and doctors weren't coming to the records office to sign them—which prevented the hospital from billing patients for millions of dollars worth of healthcare services. To meet this challenge, Janet held a creative problem-solving session and asked employees, "How can we get MDs to sign their records?" During the session, employees observed that the records office was far from where doctors typically congregated: the lounge. The solution: They put a desk outside the lounge and rewarded MDs with graham cracker cookies for signing their records. The end result: By moving a desk staffed with one employee outside the doctors' lounge, the hospital billed $4.5 million in back-logged records and has regularly reduced receivables by $3.5 million a month.

During a training session in creative problem solving, employees at a General Motors Forge Plant in upstate New York set their sights on preventing the ring gears made at their plant from sticking in and breaking dies during production—a problem that was costing the plant thousands per week. While brainstorming, one team member suggested using the cooking product PAM to prevent the sticking, and another participant quickly built on the idea. The result: Using a $1.00 spray bottle and $.50 worth of solutions, plant operators now spray the dies before making ring gears, to prevent the sticking, thus saving the plant.

When faced with the task of converting a portion of Xerox's internal business processes onto EDS's systems, EDS's Change Management Team relied heavily on creative problem-solving methods to develop a process to test and implement several major software releases. In addition, the EDS group used creativity concepts to build rapport with Xerox employees by gathering input and feedback every step of the way. The result: EDS dramatically increased Xerox's system availability and implemented their software releases without a glitch. Not only that, but EDS gathered information during each release cycle to allow for continuous improvement.

What about education? The classic Creative Studies Project, completed in 1972 at the Center for Studies in Creativity at Buffalo State College in Buffalo, New York, found that students who completed a four-semester program in creativity and innovation performed significantly better than other comparable students in coping with real-life situational tests and in applying their creative abilities in special tests given in English courses. They also performed better on the semantic and behavioral half of Guilford's structure-of-intellect model. Most students also reported large gains in their own productive creative behavior and in their ability to cope with day-to-day problems (Parnes, 1987).

In my doctoral studies I found that not only does a course in creative problem solving improve cognitive abilities (as was demonstrated by the Creative Studies Project), but training in creative problem solving also helps people work more effectively in teams. After evaluating videotapes of over forty groups in action, my findings indicated that groups trained in creative problem solving participated more, criticized ideas less, laughed more, smiled more, supported ideas more, and generated more than twice as many ideas as groups not trained in creative problem solving.

But were those extra ideas any good? When business experts evaluated the ideas for quality, they found that the groups trained in creative problem solving out-performed their counterparts by a margin of more than two to one. The final result: 618 ideas rated as excellent in the trained groups, compared to 281 excellent ideas in the untrained groups.

Finally, as a bonus, members of the trained groups indicated they enjoyed solving the problem as a group more than the untrained groups (Firestien, 1987).

There's more good news from education. More than 60 percent of our Masters of Science degree students in Creativity and Innovation at the Center for Studies in Creativity are from elementary and secondary education. These students, from all over the world, will return to their classrooms and blend their knowledge of creative problem solving with the regular school curriculum.

But the most dramatic applications of creative problem solving I have found is to save lives. Although creative problem solving is not designed as a counseling method, one of my students, a social worker, facilitated a suicidal eighteen-year-old through several phases of a creative problem-solving process. By using the brainstorming technique and the PPC approach, this young man found he had too many interesting things to do and so much to live for that it wasn't worthwhile to end his life.

Each of these changes was brought about by an innovator—someone who had the ability to envision the future not just in an abstract, daydreaming, fantasizing way, but someone who had the interest, the capability, and commitment to achieve that vision. Are you an innovator?

This fable is not just a pleasant story. These methods work. As one of my students said, "Creative problem solving helps you move from crashing around life to crafting your life."

The choice is up to you.

An Invitation

Several years ago I was asked in a seminar to look at the things in my life to which I was committed. As a result of that seminar, my commitment to others is this: "To help you apply your creativity in your world to create results." To honor that commitment I deliver speeches, conduct workshops, write books, produce audio and videotapes, consult with leaders, and train people to facilitate creative problem solving in their organizations.

Our company also publishes a quarterly newsletter, *Innovation Espresso*. The newsletter is free and is designed to keep you up-to-date on the latest work in the field of creativity and innovation. It is also a great reminder of the principles discussed in this book. If you are interested in receiving information on programs in creative problem solving that my organization delivers, or if you want to receive *Innovation Espresso*, please contact me at the following address:

Dr. Roger L. Firestien
Innovation Resources, Inc.
P.O. Box 615
Williamsville, NY 14231-0615
Voice: 716-631-3564
Fax: 716-631-2610
www.RogerFirestien.com

References

Bach, R. *Illusions: Adventures of a Reluctant Messiah*. New York: Delacorte Press/Eleanor Friede, (1977).

Campbell, D. *Take the Road to Creativity and Get Off Your Dead End*. Greensboro, NC: Center for Creative Leadership, (1985).

de Bono, E. *Lateral Thinking for Management*. New York: American Management Association, (1971).

Firestien, R. *Effects of Creative Problem Solving Training on Communication Behaviors and Quality of Ideas Generated in Small Groups*. (Doctoral dissertation, State University of New York at Buffalo, Dissertation Abstracts International, 48, 4805-A, (1987).

Firestien, R. *From Basics to Breakthroughs*. Williamsville, NY: Innovation Systems Group, (1988).

Firestien, R. *Leading on the Creative Edge*. Colorado Springs, CO: Pinön Press, (1997).

Firestien, R. *Power Think*. Williamsville, NY: Innovation Systems Group, (1987).

Osborn, A.F. *Applied Imagination*. New York: Scribners and Sons, (1963).

Note: The PPC was originally developed in the early 1980s by Diane Foucar-Szocki, Bill Shepard, and Roger Firestien.

Other Resources by Roger L. Firestien, Ph.D.

From Basics to Breakthroughs
A Guide to Better Thinking and Decision Making
Two-cassette program with guidebook

Power Think
Achieving Your Goals Through Mental Rehearsal
Audio cassette tape

Breakthrough: Getting Better Ideas
Seven Ways to Jump-Start Your Creativity
Audio cassette tape

Unleashing the Power of Creativity
Video Training Program
40-minute video with facilitator manual

Leading on the Creative Edge
Gaining Competitive Advantage through the Power
of Creative Problem Solving
200-page book

Available from
Roger L. Firestien, Ph.D.
Innovation Resources, Inc.
P.O. Box 615
Williamsville, NY 14231-0615
(Tel) 716-631-3564   (Fax)716-631-2610
www.RogerFirestien.com